# HOW TO PREPARE YOUR OWN

# LAST WILL

## AND

# TESTAMENT

**WRITTEN BY ERIC J. STERN, ATTORNEY AT LAW**

© COPYRIGHT 1993 Eric J. Stern

* **A BRIEF AND EASY TO UNDERSTAND GUIDE FOR DRAFTING YOUR OWN WILL.**

* **VALID IN ALL 50 STATES AND WASHINGTON D.C.**

* **INCLUDES TWO SETS OF FORMS FOR A LAST WILL AND TESTAMENT.**

* **EXPLAINS HOW TO PREPARE A LETTER OF INSTRUCTIONS.**

* **HELPS YOU TO PROVIDE A GUARDIAN FOR YOUR MINOR CHILDREN.**

* **ASSISTS YOU IN DEVELOPING AN INVENTORY OF YOUR ASSETS.**

* **THIS KIT WILL HELP YOU ELIMINATE OR REDUCE THE LEGAL COSTS OF PREPARING A WILL.**

## FORWARD

In order to properly create a Will with this Kit, it is strongly suggested you read the entire contents completely before trying to complete any of the forms.

## ABOUT THE AUTHOR

Eric J. Stern is a graduate of Brooklyn Law School. He practices law in the State and Federal Courts of New York and New Jersey. Mr. Stern donates pro bono time to write Wills for the terminally ill. He is presently at work on a further volume for this series which will cover the area of Health Care Proxies.

## NOTICE

### BY USING THIS LEGAL KIT, YOU ARE ACTING AS YOUR OWN ATTORNEY.

The publishers and authors are not liable for the material included in this publication. The use of this book and its forms constitutes a waiver by the buyer of all legal action against the publishers, authors and their associates. This product is warranted only to the purchase price.

# TABLE OF CONTENTS

| | |
|---|---|
| Purpose of Book | ii |
| Forward | iii |
| About the Author | iii |
| Notice (Disclaimer) | iii |
| Table of Contents | iv |
| INTRODUCTION | 1 |
| BACKGROUND | 1 |
| WILL SUBSTITUTES | 1 |
| PROFESSIONAL REVIEW | 1 |
| CONSIDERATIONS FOR MARRIED INDIVIDUALS | 2 |
| CONSIDERATIONS FOR PERSONS WITH CHILDREN | 2 |
| HOW LONG IS A WILL VALID | 4 |
| WHERE TO KEEP YOUR WILL | 4 |
| WHAT PROPERTY TO DISTRIBUTE | 5 |
| THE SAMPLE PROPERTY LIST FORM | 6 |
| THE SAMPLE WILL FORM | 13 |
| THE WITNESS VERIFICATION PAGE | 18 |
| LETTERS OF INSTRUCTION | 19 |
| DIRECTIONS FOR COMPLETING FORMS | 20 |
| GLOSSARY | 22 |
| FINAL THOUGHTS BEFORE YOU BEGIN | 23 |
| BLANK FORMS | 24 |
| Appendix (Other Legal Kits) | 37 |

# INTRODUCTION

The purpose of a Will is to provide you with a clear picture of how you want your possessions distributed.

Our aim is to assist you in determining what assets you have and how to best express your intentions for their allocation.

# BACKGROUND

### WHAT RESULTS IF YOU DIE INTESTATE?

The term "intestate" refers to the state of being without a Will.

The legislators of the various states of our country have created provisions in their laws to insure that should a person die without a will, those persons most closely related would receive that individual's property both real and personal, which is what is meant when we refer to an estate. The problem with these laws is that they do not provide for relations who are not obvious to your local legislature. Thus friends, fiancée, family members, and social organizations, all of whom you would otherwise want to see receive gifts from your estate will be left out if you fail to leave a Will.

### "WILL SUBSTITUTES"

Most states have statutes to assist a potential donor in making a gift. Two common examples of this are: *BANK ACCOUNTS* with specific survivorship provisions and *INSURANCE POLICIES* which allow the purchaser of the policy to name their own beneficiaries.

Since these types of property come clearly labeled with how you wish to have them assigned, they are generally not affected by your Will. These so-called "Will substitutes" are fine, but like the state law provisions for people who die intestate, these remedies probably won't cover many of those people to whom you want to give your property.

### REVIEWING THIS WILL WITH PROFESSIONALS

It is always a good idea to contact an attorney both to review your will and to find out the specific details of the laws of your state. The Will form enclosed was designed to satisfy the laws of all fifty states, but is not directed at the law consequences you as an individual may face. If your estate is larger than $100,000.00 or you have been giving gifts of $10,000.00 or more per year to any one individual, it is strongly recommended you seek legal and tax advice to fit your particular situation.

# CONSIDERATIONS FOR MARRIED INDIVIDUALS

Although this kit is not intended to help in tax planning, it should be noted that under current law after the payment of all bills and costs related to the administration of your affairs, your spouse can be given 100% of your estate, without any Federal Estate Taxes. Many states also have provisions which allow a spouse to gift his or her property to their marital partner without any taxes. This benefit should be strongly considered when you make out your Will.

In an effort to protect married persons from the potentially harmful effects of being disinherited by their spouses, almost every state has adopted a statute requiring that a specified minimum percentage of the individual estate be given to their spouse. These states can be broken up into three separate groups Common Law states and Community Property states and Louisiana, which is governed by a special civil code.

The Community Property states include Arizona, California, Idaho, Nevada, New Mexico, Texas, Washington, and although it does not use the exact same terms, Wisconsin. In states which have adopted the theory of community property, any property obtained after the marriage is considered to be community property, unless the after acquired property was obtained as a gift given specifically to one spouse, as in the case of an inheritance. Thus an individual is free to dispose of their one half interest in all property obtained by the couple after the marriage and all of the property which they possessed prior to the marriage. It should be noted that property owned by the spouse prior to the marriage can become community property either by virtue of the use of community funds to improve or maintain the property, or by virtue of a gift or agreement entered into with the intent of making the item community property.

The Common Law states include all other states except Louisiana.

Louisiana residents should refer to the Louisiana Civil code which has detailed provisions relating to the protection of spouses and children from disinheritance.

The Common Law states are unfortunately not consistent and thus we will be breaking them down into groups which have similar provisions. In order to make locating your states requirements somewhat easier, an alphabetical list of states will follow each type of provision.

The following states require that you provide your spouse with at least one/third of the testator's property, which is calculated by including not only the property set forth in the Will, but also property distributed under Will substitutes such as joint-tenancies and trusts:

Alabama, Alaska, Maine, Montana, Nebraska, New Jersey, North Dakota, and South Dakota. The law in Colorado is similar as it requires that one/half of all of the testator's property to be provided to the testator's spouse.

The following states require that the Will provide the testator's spouse with one/third of his or her real property for the rest of the spouses' life: Connecticut, District Of Columbia, Kentucky, Rhode Island, South Carolina, Vermont, Virginia, and West Virginia.

The following states have slightly more complicated statutes which provide that the surviving spouse receive one-half of the estate, unless there are children in which case the spouse is to receive one-third of the estate: Illinois, Kansas, Maryland, Massachusetts, Michigan, Minnesota, Mississippi, Missouri, New Hampshire, New York, North Carolina, Ohio, and Oklahoma. The provisions for these states can be complicated and it is highly recommended that you review your local statutes.

Arkansas provides the spouse with a life interest in one third of the personal and real property of the estate.

Delaware provides the surviving spouse with the lesser of either one third of the estate or $20,000.00.

Florida provides a surviving spouse with the right to at least 30% of the estate.

Oregon provides the surviving spouse with the right to at least one fourth of the estate.

# CONSIDERATIONS FOR PERSONS WITH CHILDREN

As set forth above every state has a required minimum which must be provided to the testator's surviving spouse. With the exception of Louisiana, no other state requires that you make any gift at all to your other family members. The general rule is that an individual should at least mention the names of his or her surviving children derived from children who are deceased. The following states have relatively complex regulations regarding family members who should be mentioned in the Will and thus local statutes should be referred to: Georgia, Nevada, Oregon, South Dakota, Washington, and Wyoming.

If you do not wish to leave anything to your child, then you should do so by clearly naming the child and stating that you do not desire for this child to inherit from your estate. Many states treat grandchildren who survive their parents, in the same way as children and thus they should also be directly named and provided for. For the purposes of most statutes adopted children are treated in the same manner as one's own biological children, and again they should be expressly named and either given a bequest or disinherited.

## WHO CAN HAVE A WILL

Every adult who is capable enough to know what property they have and to whom they wish to give the property to can make a Will. The standards for judging the capacity to make a Will are relatively flexible. Unless there is a party actually contesting the capacity of the individual who made the Will most courts will assume that the testator was capable of making an effective gift of his or her property.

The minimum age requirement for making an effective Will is 14 years of age in Georgia, 16 years of age in Louisiana, 21 years of age in New Jersey, and 18 years of age in all other states.

Maine, New Hampshire and Texas have exceptions which allow married persons under the minimum age to make a Will. Indiana makes a similar exception for persons in the armed forces and the merchant marine.

## SPECIAL CONSIDERATIONS FOR PERSONS RESIDING IN LOUISIANA

The Laws of Louisiana derive from the French Civil Code and they are different from those of the other 49 states. When you have completed filling in the scrap copy of the Will form, you must make arrangements with the District Court Clerk for your local Parish to dictate your Will to him or her in the presence of three witnesses. This will require some special changes in the exact phrasing of the Will at both the introductory paragraph and the closing paragraph. You should be able to get the exact language for these paragraphs from either the office of the District Clerk for your Parish or from local counsel.

# HOW LONG IS A WILL VALID

Once your Will has been executed it is valid until you either destroy it or prepare a new one. It is important to eliminate your old Will after you have made a replacement. The reason is that otherwise there may be confusion as to which is valid and even if that is not a factor, persons who are disinherited could use the prior Will as a basis for a legal challenge of the new document. Remember the clearer things appear in Surrogate's Court the better if is for those whom you intend to give a benefit.

# WHERE TO KEEP YOUR WILL

Once completed you should keep your Will in a safe place. It is best to have your attorney keep your Will in his office. This is because attorneys and their records are usually easy to locate. As a prerequisite to practicing law in almost every state an attorneys is required to leave their forwarding addresses with the state's attorney licensing board. If you don't have an attorney, you can contact your local Probate Court and, in many parts of the county, they will accept the original for filing, for a small fee. The drawback to this is that if you should create a new Will, confusion could result.

It is suggested you do not use your own bank's safety deposit box as a repository for your Will. Should you do so you may create unwanted difficulties for those who are to assist with your estate. In order to open up a deceased persons safety deposit box a U.S. Treasury agent is required to be present at its opening for the purposes of protecting the Federal government's interest in the estate of the departed. While the potential delays are substantial, it is certainly not the worst location for your Will if you can find no other safe place to leave it.

# WHAT PROPERTY TO DISTRIBUTE

In determining what assets you have it is a good idea to concentrate on what you would have available for sale, if you had to raise money for an emergency.

It is suggested that you prepare a list of the tangible and intangible property you own. The list provided includes a place for you to put a complete description of every item involved including serial numbers, a replacement value, and an explanation of how you obtained the replacement value, and the person to whom you wish the property to be delivered upon your death. Remember to include a telephone number, where available, with every address requested in the form.

The advantage of using the property list is that it can be used by you or your family to provide information for insurance and police reports. A copy of this list should be provided to your executor as it will help your executor to locate your property and place a valuation on your estate. It will also help guide your executor in distributing property not otherwise provided for in the Will.

The authors of this text do not advise you use this property list to supplement your Will. Should you choose to do so the list must be executed with all the formalities of a Will and may not be altered once it is executed. If it is not executed with the same formalities as a will, it may not be binding upon your executor, and it will be merely advisory.

A tear out sample PROPERTY LIST FORM is provided as a guide on the following pages:

SAMPLE PROPERTY LIST FORM

# PROPERTY LIST

Estate of: *John William Smith*

Residing at: *123 Main Street*

*Deer Park, NY*

Date this list was last updated: *January 15, 1990*

## 1. Real Estate

### a. Residence:

Address and or description: *123 Main Street*

*Deer Park, NY*

Market value: $ *$210,000.00*    How value was arrived at: *Given Associates Real Estate Appraisers*

Amount of any known mortgage or lien and the name and address of any party which has a mortgage, lien, or other interest in the property: *None*

### b. Other Interests In Real Property:

Address or description: *House at 400 Pond Road*

*Southampton, NY*

Market value: $ *275,000.00*    How Value was arrived at: *Given Associates Real Estate Appraisers*.

Amount of any known mortgage or lien and the name and address of the party who has a mortgage, lien, or other interest in property: *$60,000.00 mortgage with Norstar Bank, 710 Montauk Highway, Southampton, NY*

Name and address of person or persons whom you wish to receive this property upon your death: *Southampton house to Patricia Smith Wilson of 222 Fifth Ave., New York City, NY*

*Deer Park house to Robert Edward Smith of 59 Franklin Ave., Garden City, NY*.

SAMPLE PROPERTY LIST (CONT.)

2. **Stocks, Bonds, Loans** Owing To The Estate

   a.) Address and description: *Lynch Etc., 50 Route 111, Hauppauge, NY*
   *250 Shares AT common stock worth $21,000.00 ; 150 shares IE common stock worth $42,000.00 ; 100 shares General Class B Preferred worth $68,000.00*

   Market Value: $ *131,000.00*   How determined: *Street Journal NYSE*

   Name and address of any party with an interest or lien on the property, including a description of the parties' interest: *None*

   Name and address of person you wish to receive this property upon your death:
   *Robert Edward Smith of 59 Franklin Ave., Garden City, NY*

   b.) Address and description: _____

   Market Value: $ _____  How determined: _____

   Name and address of any party with an interest or lien on the property, including a description of the parties' interest: _____

   Name and address of person you wish to receive this property upon your death: _____

3. **Life Insurance And Employee Benefits**

   a.) Type of insurance: *Whole Life Insurance*

   Market Value: $ *50,000.00*   How determined: *Face Value on paid up policy*

   Name of insurance company: *Life Insurance Company*

   Name and address of your insurance broker, or the company representative who handles insurance claims at your company: *Lawrence Johnston, 350 Veterans Memorial Hwy, Commack, NY 11725*

## SAMPLE PROPERTY LIST (CONT.)

If you have borrowed against this policy give an explanation including amount borrowed, and location of all related records: _____

_____

Name and address of all beneficiaries: _____

_____

_____

b.) Type of insurance or benefit: _____

Market Value: $_____ How determined: _____

_____

Name of insurance company: _____
Name and address of your insurance broker, or the company representative who handles insurance claims at your company: _____

_____

_____

If you have borrowed against this policy give an explanation including amount borrowed, and location of all related records: _____

_____

Name and address of all beneficiaries: _____

_____

_____

**4. Interests in vehicles**

a.) Type of vehicle: *1992 Buick Roadmaster sedan*

_____

Vehicle identification number: *GV 8294576916*
Market value: $ *22,000.00* How Determined: *Blue Book*

_____

This vehicle insured by: *Farm Insurance*
Name and address of person to whom you desire to inherit this vehicle: _____
*Matthew John Smith of 123 Main Street, Deer Park, NY*

_____

If you have a loan on the vehicle or share ownership with another person, so state, and provide an explanation of such interest including the location of all related records:

## SAMPLE PROPERTY LIST (CONT.)

b.) Type of vehicle: _____

Vehicle identification number: _____

Market value: $_____  How Determined: _____

This vehicle insured by: _____
Name and address of person to whom you desire to inherit this vehicle: _____

If you have a loan on the vehicle or share ownership with another person, so state, and provide an explanation of such interest including the location of all related records:

_____

## 5. Bank Accounts

a.) Type of account: *Checking*
Account number: *2218-10-6873*
Name and address of Bank: *National Bank, 328 Deer Park Ave., Deer Park, NY*

Estimated value: *$1800.00*
Name and address of any beneficiary or co-owner of account: *Patricia Smith Wilson of 222 Fifth Ave., New York City, NY*

If you have a lien or pledge against the account, so state, and provide an explanation of such interest including the location of all documentation related thereto: *None*

b.) Type of account: *Savings*
Account number: *899930442*
Name and address of Bank: *Savings Bank, HuntingtonSquare Mall, East Northport, NY*

## SAMPLE PROPERTY LIST (CONT)

Estimated value: *$1500.00*

Name and address of any beneficiary or co-owner of account: *None*

If you have a lien or pledge against the account, so state, and provide an explanation of such interest including the location of all documentation related thereto:

### 6. Safe Deposit Boxes

Name and address of the Bank which contains your safe deposit box:
*Savings Bank, Huntington Sq. Mall, East Northport, NY*

Number of your safe deposit: *1209345*

Name and address of any party other than yourself with access to this depository:
*Matthew John Smith of 123 Main Street, Deer Park, NY*

Name and address of person or persons you want to receive contents of the safe deposit box upon your death: *Matthew John Smith of 123 Main Street, Deer Park, NY*

### 7. Other Property

a.) Description of property: *Stamp and Coin Collections and 2 Season Tickets to the New York Giants Football Team*

Location of property: *Safe Deposit Box 1209345 at Savings Bank, Huntington Sq. Mall*

Name of person who has possession of property:

Name and address of any party who has an interest in the property:

Value of property: $ *2000.00*   How Determined: *Current Selling Price in NY Times*

Location of any documents relating to your ownership of the property:
*Tickets and Contract in Safe deposit box.*

Name and address of person or persons whom you wish to receive this property upon your death: *Ernie Scott of 93 Underhill Street, Syosset, NY*

## SAMPLE PROPERTY LIST (CONT)

b.) Description of property: *Ping Golf Clubs*

Location of property: *basement*

Name of person who has possession of property: _____

Name and address of any party who has an interest in the property: _____

Value of property: $ *1200.00*   How Determined: *Purchase price*

Location of any documents relating to your ownership of the property:
*Receipt and Warranty in desk drawer*

Name and address of person or persons whom you wish to receive this property upon your death: *Marty Jack Nickels of 250 Campbell Street, Dix Hills, NY*

c.) Description of property: *Golf Cart Serial No. MR187253*

Location of property: *Half Hollow Hills Country Club*

Name of person who has possession of property: *Walter Madden, Club Manager*

Name and address of any party who has an interest in the property: _____

Value of property: $ *2100.00*   How Determined: *Purchase Price*

Location of any documents relating to your ownership of the property: *Receipt and Title in desk drawer.*

Name and address of person or persons whom you wish to receive this property upon your death: *Marty Jack Nickels of 250 Campbell Street, Dix Hills, NY*

## SUGGESTIONS FOR COMPLETING PROPERTY LIST FORM

Some suggestions for what types of property you may wish to consider including are as follows:

Real Property - Any interest you have in a house, co-operative, or condominium should be considered in your Will.

Vehicles - cars, trucks, boats, snowmobiles, airplanes, or motorcycles.

Collections - books, pictures, rare coins, china sets, silverware, record collections, stamps, baseball cards, autographs, videotapes, etc.

Household Furnishings - antiques, lamps, rugs, television sets, videotape players, furniture, home computers, stereo equipment, appliances, tools, etc.

Business related Property - Inventory, tools and equipment related to the operation of a business. Keep in mind your interest in a business may also be an asset of your estate.

Pets or farm animals - Keep in mind the value of the animals, including breeding rights.

Intangibles - Interests you may have in a lawsuit, film, play, book, trademark, patent, song, right of recovery on a debt, or other intangible.

# THE SAMPLE WILL FORM

On the following pages you will find a copy of a Will form. On the right side of each page is a portion of the form. Wherever there is a blank space a number appears. On the left side of each page the number will be repeated followed by a short description of what type of information belongs in that blank space. If you read the comments which follow on the left hand side, you will find some suggestions which you may find helpful.

At the end of the form you will see that there is space for three witnesses to provide their name, address, and signature. The following seven states actually require three witnesses:
Louisiana, Maine, Massachusetts, New Hampshire, Pennsylvania, South Carolina, and Vermont. It is recommended that you have three witnesses even if it is not required by your state. The reason for this suggestion is that the extra individual could prove useful, if testimony on the execution of the Will becomes necessary.

The witnesses should be individuals who are over the age of twenty-one. They should not be persons who are receiving any gifts under the Will. While more than a dozen states such as Alabama, Idaho, and Maryland, allow witnesses to receive gifts under a Will, it is strongly recommended that you avoid this practice as it raises questions involving the potential for conflicting interests. An additional consideration to keep in mind when choosing potential witnesses is to try to choose persons who would be easy to locate, if their testimony were to become necessary. If possible it is a good idea to keep track of the addresses for your witnesses and to put this information in your letter of instructions to your executor.

Most states provide for the possibility of a "self-proving affidavit". This affidavit, a copy of which is provided after the last page of the Will form provided herein, allows the testator and the witnesses to swear before a notary public as to the manner in which the Will was executed. This may reduce the need for the Court to obtain an appearance from the witnesses at the time of probate. Obviously, the best way to handle this is to have a notary public present at the time the Will is executed. The following states do not yet recognize the "self-proving affidavit": California, Maryland, Michigan, Ohio, Vermont, Wisconsin, and Washington D.C..

Read the form very carefully, and write out everything on the worksheets provided with this kit before filling the form in. You should pay special attention to the provision in paragraph Nine which deals with appointing a Guardian for your minor children. Obviously the other parent ordinarily has the right to raise your children regardless of what you provide. However, single parents and persons considering the possibility of the death of both parents before their children's coming of age should seriously consider who they want to see raise their children. If you use a person outside of your immediate family, your choice may be challenged. It is a good idea to try to talk to parties whom you would be expected to choose, but have decided against, so as to avoid the hurt feelings which may result from your decision.

(1) & (2) Place the full name of the person making the Will in this space.

(3) Place the full address of the residence of the person making the Will in this space. Remember your residence is the home at which you live the majority of the year.

(4) County in which you make your residence.

(5) City or Township in which you make your residence.

(6) State in which you make your residence.

(7) Name the item of property which you intend to give the individual. It is recommended that you put your gifts to your spouse and your children early in the Will. If you choose to disinherit a child, then state your intention in this blank. Remember you must eventually name your spouse and all of your children in the Will. Paragraph Three is broken up into seven Sections marked by letters A through G, thus you can use this paragraph to make gifts to as many as seven individuals.

Remember when listing your property to be clear as to what it is you intend to give. For example, if you want the person named to receive your "1988 Lincoln Continental" then so state. If however, you want the person to receive whatever car it is you have at the time of your death, then simply set forth that you wish they receive your automobile and don't specify the make. Keep in mind your property is likely to change, so you should make it plain if it is a particular item you wish to give, or a general type of property.

## LAST WILL AND TESTAMENT
## OF

*John William Smith*
(1)

I, *John William Smith*
(2)

residing at *123 Main Street*
(3)

*Deer Park*, in the County of *Suffolk*,
(3) (4)

City or Township of *Babylon*, State of *New York*, do hereby make,
(5) (6)

publish and declare the following as and for my LAST WILL AND TESTAMENT

FIRST: I hereby revoke any and all wills and codicils by me at any time heretofore made.

SECOND: I direct my Executor to pay out of my estate as an expense of administration, without apportionment, all estate, death, transfer, succession, inheritance, legacy, and similar taxes by whatever name called, including interest and penalties thereon, which may be assessed or imposed under the laws of any jurisdiction by reason of my death, upon or with respect to any property passing under this my LAST WILL AND TESTAMENT.

THIRD: (A) I give *the house and contents at 123 Main Street*,
(7)

*Deer Park, NY*, to my *son*, *Robert Edward Smith*, currently
(8) (9)

residing at *59 Franklin Avenue, Garden City, NY*.
(10)

(B) I give *the house and contents at 400 Pond Road,*
(7)

*Southampton, NY*, to my *daughter*, *Patricia Smith Wilson*, currently
(8) (9)

residing at *222 Fifth Avenue, New York City, NY*.
(10)

(C) I give *my 1992 Buick Roadmaster sedan*
(7)

to my *grandson*, *Matthew John Smith*, currently residing at *123 Main Street*,
(8) (9) (10)

*Deer Park, NY*.

(D) I give *my golf clubs and golf cart*,
(7)

to my *caddy*, *Marty Jack Nickels*, currently residing at *250 Campbell Street*,
(8) (9) (10)

*Dix Hills, NY*.

(E) I give *my stocks and bonds holdings in my Merrill Lynch Account*
(7)

to my *son*, *Robert Edward Smith*, currently residing at *59 Franklin Avenue,*
(8) (9) (10)

*Garden City, NY*.

(F) I give *my set of 2 season tickets to the New York Giants Football Team*
(7)

to my *friend*, *Ernie Scott* currently residing at *93 Underhill Street*,
(8) (9) (10)

*Syosset, NY*.

14

(G) I give _my entire stamp and coin collections_ to my _nephew_ , _Jay Smith_ , currently residing at _625 Flagg Street_ , _Denver, Colorado_ .

**In** Paragraph Three Section (H) of the Will you are disposing of your personal property other than money.

(H) I give all (other) tangible personal property owned by me at the time of my death, including but not limited to all articles of personal and household use or ornament, including articles (not effectively disposed of under the foregoing provisions), to my _daughter_ , _Patricia Smith Wilson_ , currently residing at 222 Fifth Avenue New York , NY . In the event that the aforementioned _Particia Smith Wilson_ should predecease me or refuse their gift, then I give all said tangible personal property to my _son_ , _Robert Edward Smith_ , currently residing at _59 Franklin Avenue , Garden City, NY_ .

FOURTH: (A) I give to my _nephew_ , _Thomas Gary Smith_ , who currently resides at _65 Apple Lane , Lake Grove , NY_ , the sum of _Five Thousand_ dollars ($ _5,000.00_).

(B) I give to my _niece_ , _Teena Susan Smith_ , who currently resides at _55 Apple Lane , Lake Grove , NY_ , the sum of _Five Thousand_ , dollars ($_5,000.00_).

(C) I give to my _sister_ , _Carol-Lee Smith Jones_ , who currently resides at _75 Apple Lane , Lake Grove , NY_ , the sum of _Ten Thousand_ , dollars ($_10,000.00_).

(D) I give to my _____ , _____ , who currently resides at _____ , the sum of _____ , dollars ($_____).

(E) I give to my _____ , _____ , who currently resides at _____ , the sum of _____ , dollars ($_____).

(F) I give to my _____ , _____ , who currently resides at _____ , the sum of _____ , dollars ($_____).

**P**aragraph Five describes the manner in which you wish to dispose of the residuary estate.

**Y**our residuary estate includes whatever is left over of the estate after all expenses have been paid and the gifts described above have been given.

FIFTH: The remainder of my estates both real and personal, and wheresoever situated, of which I may have title possession at the time of my death, or to which I may be in any way entitled, which shall be referred to as my "residuary estate," I give to my __daughter__ <sub>(23)</sub>, __Patricia Smith Wilson__ <sub>(24)</sub>, currently residing at __222 Fifth Avenue , New York , NY__ <sub>(25)</sub>. In the event the aforementioned should predecease me or refuse this gift, then I give my residuary estate to my __son__ <sub>(27)</sub>, __Robert Edward Smith__ <sub>(28)</sub>, currently residing at __59 Franklin Avenue , Garden City , NY__ <sub>(29)</sub>.

SIXTH: I direct that the arrangements for the disposition of my body be as follows: __have a Catholic service and burial at Pinelawn National Cemetary, Pinelawn, NY__ <sub>(30)</sub>. I further direct that my funeral be carried out under the directions of my executor, __Robert Edward Smith__ <sub>(31)</sub>.

SEVENTH: I direct that no bond or other security shall be required in any jurisdiction of any fiduciary, including a preliminary executor, appointed hereunder for any cause whatsoever, including the advance payment of commissions.

In Paragragh Eight you will be selecting an Executor who will oversee the distribution of your estate.

It is recommended that this person be both trustworthy and reliable, as it is this person who will be working to settle your estate.

EIGHTH: I hereby nominate __Robert Edward Smith__ <sub>(32)</sub> currently residing at __59 Franklin Avenue , Garden City, NY__ <sub>(33)</sub>, as the Executor of this my LAST WILL AND TESTAMENT. In the event the aforementioned is unable to serve, or ceases to serve, then I nominate __Patricia Smith Wilson__ <sub>(34)</sub>, currently residing at __222 Fifth Avenue , New York City, NY__ <sub>(35)</sub>, as the alternate Executor of this my LAST WILL AND TESTAMENT.

In Paragragh Nine you will be appointing a guardian for you minor children.

Keep in mind the problems discussed in the main body of the text.

NINTH: I hereby nominate __Carol-Lee Smith Jones__ <sub>(36)</sub> currently residing at __75 Apple Lane,__ <sub>(37)</sub> , __Lake Grove , NY__ <sub>(38)</sub>, as the Guardian of the person and property of any minor child of mine. In the event the aforementioned __Carol-Lee Smith Jones__ <sub>(39)</sub>, should become unable to serve as Guardian, then I nominate __Phillip James Smith__ <sub>(40)</sub>, who resides at __100 Sandy Beach Road , Boca Raton , Florida__ <sub>(41)</sub> as the alternative Guardian of the person and property of any minor child of mine.

TENTH: Any property passing hereunder to a minor may be distributed to a guardian of the person or property of such minor appointed in any jurisdiction, or to a custodian of the property of such minor under the Uniform Gifts or Transfers to Minors Act of any State, or to a parent of such minor, or to a person with whom such minor resides or who has control or custody of such minor, as my Executor may determine. If payment is made to a custodian, my Executor may act as the custodian or may select another custodian. The receipt of any such guardian, custodian, or parent or other person to whom any such distribution is made shall completely release and discharge my Executor with respect thereto and my Executor shall be under no further liability, responsibility or application or disposition thereof.

The next section, paragraphs **ELEVENTH** and **TWELFTH** of the Will describes the manner in which the Will was executed.

ELEVENTH : My executor and alternate Executor shall have all the express and implied powers granted to Executors by the laws of the state in which probate occurs in effect at the time of my death.

TWELFTH: If any beneficiary shall not survive me, any legacy hereunder to that beneficiary shall lapse, unless this Will shall provide otherwise.

*John William Smith*
Testator's Signature

IN WITNESS WHEREOF, I, *John William Smith* (42) ,
have to this day my LAST WILL AND TESTAMENT, consisting of *nine* (9) pages, up to and (43)
including this page, subscribed my name at the end hereof this *20th* day of *August*, 1992. (44)
The foregoing instrument was subscribed, sealed, published and declared by
*John William Smith* (45) , the Testator, as and for (his/her) LAST WILL AND TESTAMENT,
in our presence and in the presence of each of us, and we, at the same time, in (his/her) presence and in the presence of each other, having hereunto subscribed our names and residences as attesting witnesses this
*20th* day of *August* , 1992 .

| | | |
|---|---|---|
| *Joseph Rogers* (47) | residing at | *125 Main Street* (48) |
| | | *Deer Park, NY* |
| *Moreen Brown* (47) | residing at | *200 Main Street* (48) |
| | | *Deer Park, NY* |
| *Timothy Roth* (47) | residing at | *23 South Avenue* (48) |
| | | *Huntington, NY* |

Testator

# WITNESS VERIFICATION PAGE

STATE OF __New York__

COUNTY OF __Suffolk__

    We the undersigned, being duly sworn, depose and say:

    1. We witnessed the execution of the foregoing Will, dated __August 20__,19__92__ , of the Testator
(51)
__John William Smith__ . Said Testator
(52)
subscribed said Will at the end thereof at the following address:
__123 Main Street, Deer Park, NY__ , in our
(53)
presence. At the time of making such subscription, the said Testator declared such instrument so subscribed by (him/~~her~~) to be (his/~~her~~) Will, and we thereupon signed our names as witness at the end of said instrument, at the request of said Testator, and in (his/~~her~~) presence and in the presence of each other.

    2. In the opinion of each of the undersigned:

(A) The said Testator at the time of executing said instrument was over the age of eighteen (18) years, of sound mind, memory and understanding, and not under any restraint or in any respect incompetent to make a will.

(B) The said Testator could read, write and converse in the English language and was suffering from no defect of sight, hearing or speech, or from any other physical or mental impairment which would affect (his/~~her~~) capacity to make a valid Will.

3. Each of the undersigned was acquainted with said Testator, and we make this affidavit at the request of said Testator.

4. The said instrument was executed by said Testator and each of the undersigned, as witness, under the supervision of the Testator.

Testator: _____ (54)

Severally sworn to before me this
__22nd__ day of __August__ , 19__92__

Witness: _____ (55)

Witness: _____ (55)

_____
Notary Public

Witness: _____ (55)

18

# LETTERS OF INSTRUCTION:

A Letter of Instruction is an informal document which enables the Testator to provide the executor of his estate with instructions which for one reason or another are either too personal to put in a Will or were not decided upon at the time the Will was made. Letters of Instruction are not binding upon the executor and are merely there to help advise the executor.

The Letter of Instruction may be in the form of either a personal letter or a business letter addressed to your executor and may include:

1. A copy of the personal property list and the addresses of beneficiaries or witnesses who have moved since you made the Will. This will simplify the administration of the estate considerably.

2. The location of the Will or of property involved in the estate. Since you want to make your executor's job to be as easy as is possible it is important to tell him/her the name of the institutions with whom you have placed accounts, safety deposit boxes, insurance, or other property. In addition, you should follow this with the address and phone number of the organization, the name or number by which they identify your account, and the name of the person or persons with whom you have dealt with in the past.

3. A list of instructions as to funeral arrangements including persons, you, the Testator, want to have notified of your death. Remember to include the names, addresses, and phone numbers of those you want contacted.

4. Specific instructions as to the raising of your minor children living at the time of your death.

5. The location of your income tax returns, both State and Federal.

6. Instructions as to how you want personal property with mainly sentimental value, rather than material value, distributed. An example of this would be a note telling your executor to let your family member distribute you photograph albums amongst themselves.

7. Any general desires you may have for your friends and family.

**Do not use our Letter of Instructions to amend your Will. If you wish to amend your Will, it is best that you create a new Will. It is not recommended that you create a codicil to your Will. A codicil is an amendment to your Will which must be executed with the same formalities as a Will. Because of the potential for conflicts between a Will and its Codicil, it is suggested that you simply create a new Will rather than open the door to potential problems.**

# DIRECTIONS FOR COMPLETING WILL FORM

Complete blank Form in back of book using sample Form and these directions as a guide.

(1) & (2) Place the full name of the person making the Will in this space.

(3) Place the full address of the residence of the person making the Will in this space. Remember your residence is the home at which you live the majority of the year.

(4) County in which you make your residence.

(5) City or Township in which you make your residence.

(6) State in which you make your residence.

(7) Name the item of property which you intend to give the individual. It is recommended that you put your gifts to your spouse and your children early in the Will. If you choose to disinherit a child, then state your intention in this blank. Remember you must eventually name your spouse and all of your children in the Will. Paragraph Third is broken up into seven Sections marked by letters A through G, thus you can use this paragraph to make gifts to as many as seven individuals.

Remember when listing your property to be clear as to what it is you intend to give. For example, if you want the person named to receive your "1988 Lincoln Continental" then so state. If however, you want the person to receive whatever car it is you have at the time of your death, then simply set forth that you wish they receive your automobile and don't specify the make. Keep in mind your property is likely to change, so you should make it plain if it is a particular item you wish to give, or a general type of property.

(8) State your relationship to the individual. Example "son", "wife", "husband", "friend", "sister", "favorite charity", or "doctor". The term you use should be specific enough to describe the person so that if two people you know have the same name, there will not be any confusion.

(9) State the name of the person to whom you are giving this gift.

(10) Provide the address of the person to whom you are giving this gift.

In the Third Paragraph Section (H) of the Will you are disposing of the remainder of your personal property other than money.

(11) State relationship to this individual. See (8) for further instructions.

(12) State the name of the person to whom you are giving this gift.

(13) Provide the address of the person to whom you are giving this gift.

(14) Repeat the name of the individual whom you list in space number (12).

(15) Provide your relationship to the individual to whom you wish this property to go, if the individual set forth in space number (12) should not be able to accept this gift.

(16) Provide the name of the individual to whom you wish this property to go, if the person set forth in space number (12) should not be able to accept this gift.

(17) Provide the residence of the individual described in spaces (15) & (16).

(18) State your relationship to the individual to whom you will be giving money. This form has enough lines for six gifts. The instructions are the same for the spaces in the Fourth Paragraph Sections (A) through (F).

(19) Provide the name of the individual to whom you wish to provide this gift of money.

(20) Provide the address of this individual to whom you wish to make this gift of money.

(21) Type out in words, not arabic numbers, the amount of money you wish to give as this gift.

(22) Fill in the number for the amount of money you wish to give as this gift.

The Fifth Paragraph describes the manner in which you wish to dispose of the residuary estate. Your residuary estate includes whatever is left over of the estate after all expenses have been paid and the gifts described above have been given.

(23) Fill in this space with a description of your relationship to the individual to whom you wish to give the residuary of your estate.

(24) Provide the name of the individual to whom you wish to give the residuary of your estate.

(25) Provide the address of the individual to whom you wish to give the residuary of the estate.

(26) Place the name of the individual you set forth in response to blank number (24) in this space.

(27) State your relationship to the individual whom you are naming as alternative beneficiary of the residuary of the estate.

(28) Provide the name of the individual you wish to name as the alternative beneficiary of the residuary of your estate.

(29) Provide the address for the individual you have listed as the alternate beneficiary of the residuary of the estate.

(30) Provide a description of the manner in which you wish to have your body disposed. For example you may state that you wish to be cremated, have a Catholic burial, or that you wish to have your remains placed in a particular location.

In the Eighth Paragraph you will be selecting an Executor who will oversee the distribution of your estate. It is recommended that this person be both trustworthy and reliable, as it is this person who will be working to settle your estate.

(31) Fill in this blank with the name of the person whom you wish to use as your Executor.

(32) Fill in this blank with the name of the person whom you wish to have appointed as Executor here.

(33) Place the address of the person whom you wish to have appointed as Executor here.

(34) In this blank place the name of the individual you wish to have appointed as the alternative Executor.

(35) Place the address of the individual you wish to appoint the alternative Executor in this space.

In the Ninth Paragraph you are appointing a guardian for your minor children. Keep in mind the problems discussed in the main body of the text.

(36) Place the individual you wish to nominate as Guardian for your minor children in this space.

(37) Place the address of the person you wish to nominate as Guardian in this space.

(38) Put the name of the person you set forth in response to blank number (36) in this space.

(40) Place the name and address of the person you wish to use as an alternate Guardian in this space.

(41) Place the address of the person you wish to use as alternate Guardian in this space.

(42) Place the name of the person making the Will in this space.

(43) Write out the number of pages in this space and place the arabic numeral in the blank which follows.

(44) Fill in this series of spaces by putting the day, month and year in the blanks provided.

(45) Place the name of the person making the Will in this space.

(46) Place the day, month, and year in the blank spaces provided here.

(47) The names of the witnesses should be signed on the line provided and printed beneath. One line is provided for each witness.

(48) The address of each witness should be placed in the lines following their names.

(49) Fill in this blank with the name of your state.

(50) Fill in this space with the name of the county in which you are executing this affidavit.

(51) Place the date you executed the will in this blank.

(52) Place the name of the person making the Will in this blank.

(53) Fill in this blank with the address of the location where the Will was signed.

(54) Fill in this blank with the signature of the person making the Will and have their name typed in the space beneath the signature line.

(55) Have each witness sign on one of the three signature lines provided by these spaces and have their names printed beneath their signatures.

# GLOSSARY

**Beneficiary:** A person or institution who receives a gift under a will or other document which provides a benefit.

**Bequest:** A gift of property made pursuant to the terms of a Will.

**Codicil:** An amendment to a Will made with the same formalities as a Will.

**Estate:** The whole of one's possessions, including all real and personal property whether tangible or intangible.

**Executor:** A person appointed under a Will to carry out the wishes of the Testator.

**Guardian:** A person who is legally responsible for the person or property of another person or legal entity.

**Heir:** A person who inherits property either under a Will or the laws of intestacy.

**Intestate:** The state of being without a legal Will.

**Joint Property:** All property owned jointly with another person or persons.

**Probate:** The legal establishment of the validity of a Will.

**Remainder:** Property in the estate left after all the specific bequests are satisfied.

**Surety Bond:** A bond agreement which insures that if the executor mishandles the estate, the losses will be covered.

**Testament:** A written document in which a person disposes of personal property in existence after his or her death.

**Testator:** A person who makes a legally valid Will.

**Witness:** A person who verifies the actions of another. In this case, the witnesses should be a person who has achieved the legal age of majority under the laws of your State, who is not a beneficiary under your will and who is competent enough to understand what is occurring.

# FINAL THOUGHTS

Now that you have read this manual through, you are ready to proceed to draft your own Will. Keep in mind that if you can't understand something, then it is very likely that those who act upon your instructions will have similar difficulties. Try to be as specific as you can and, if possible, ask someone to read everything over for you.

Remember that it is better to be as considerate as possible when you draft your Will. There is no point in using this Will to insult family members or as a device to bring people into conflict.

Don't leave any part of the Will blank. Fill any unneeded parts of the Will with the words "Not Applicable" or N.A..

Once the Will has been executed you are not to add any additional information to the Will. If it appears that material has been added to the Will after its execution, it may be grounds to have the Will set aside. There have been a large number of lawsuits over Wills which appear to have been altered after execution. Even excess staple holes in a document can give rise to the presumption of tampering. Since most states don't allow for written Wills, there should be no handwritten information in the body of the Will, except in the portions requiring a signature.

Make sure that if you intend to omit a former marital partner, that the divorce proceeding has been finalized. Recently, I have come across individuals who wanted to execute Wills excluding persons to whom they are still technically married. This can crate serious problems as the former spouse still has the right of election and can thus come in and contest the Will. While it might be unpleasant to go through divorce proceedings, it is the best course of action. Even if you can't locate your former spouse, you may still be able to complete the necessary steps to terminate your marriage. You can get more details involving this issue from attorneys in your area, divorce hotlines, the agency in your state which regulates marriage licenses, and other publications in this series. Do not simply ignore this issue.

Don't give property to pets. Give the pet to a person or an organization with a gift of money to provide for the pet. You can always put specific details as to your wishes for the care of pets in your Letter of Instructions.

Remember to talk to the people to whom you are giving responsibilities such as guardianships or executorships. Make sure they understand what you are asking them to do and that they are ready and willing to do it. Be sure to tell your executor where you are keeping your Will.

If you ultimately find that the forms contained herein are not as satisfactory as an individually drafted document prepared by a legal counselor more closely in touch with your personal needs, then use these to help formulate what you will be discussing with your legal counsel. This will let you create an outline which will allow you and your counsel to separate out those issues which easy to resolve and thus focus in on issues where you have a particular problem which would require a more detailed approach. These forms can always be used as a temporary solution until you can get to legal counsel.

Before you rule out the possibility of obtaining legal counsel, due to expense, think about the different sources of legal aid available to you. Many individuals have legal services available to them through their place of employment. Check with your employer or union representative to see what benefits you may be entitled to. Many law schools and bar associations provide low cost or free services to those who qualify. Many groups which specialize in helping particular segments of the population, based upon age, sex, national origin, religion, sexual preference, or membership in a particular social organization have legal referral programs which may be able to help. In addition several credit related services, including many credit card companies, have legal referral programs. Depending upon your circumstances, even full cost legal assistance in regards to Will preparation may not be out of reach. Since establishing the cost of assistance is only a phone call away, it is strongly recommended that you do so.

# BLANK FORMS

The following pages contain tear out blank forms for the Last Will And Testament, The Witness Verification Page, and the Property List Form.

Use the completed Sample Forms starting on page 13 and the Directions for Completing Forms starting on page 20 to carefully prepare the forms.

Two sets of blank forms are provided. It is suggested one set be used as worksheets.

# NOTES

# NOTES

# NOTES

# NOTES

# LAST WILL AND TESTAMENT
## OF

_____

I,_____

residing at_____

_____, in the County of _____

_____, City of _____, State of

_____, do hereby make, publish and declare the following as and for my LAST WILL AND TESTAMENT.

    FIRST: I hereby revoke any and all wills and codicils by me at any time heretofore made.

    SECOND: I direct my Executor to pay out of my estate as an expense of administration, without apportionment, all estate, death, transfer, succession, inheritance, legacy, and similar taxes by whatever name called, including interest and penalties thereon, which may be assessed or imposed under the laws of any jurisdiction by reason of my death, upon or with respect to any property passing under this my LAST WILL AND TESTAMENT.

    THIRD:     (A) I give_____

_____to my _____

_____, currently residing at

_____

_____.

    (B) I give_____

to my _____, _____

_____, currently residing at _____

_____.

    (C) I give _____

to my _____, _____

_____, currently residing at _____

_____.

    (D) I give _____

to my _____, _____

_____, currently residing at _____

_____

_____.

      (E) I give _____

to my _____, _____

_____, currently residing at _____

_____.

      (F) I give _____

to my _____, _____

_____, currently residing at _____

_____.

      (G) I give _____

to my _____, _____

_____, currently residing at _____

_____.

      (H) I give all (other) tangible personal property owned by me at the time of my death, including but not limited to all articles of personal and household use or ornament, including articles (not effectively disposed of under the foregoing provisions), to my _____, _____

_____, currently residing at _____

_____

_____.

In the event that the aforementioned _____

_____, should predecease me or refuse their gift, then I give all said tangible personal property to my _____,_____

_____, currently residing

at_____

   FOURTH:  (A) I give to my _____,_____

who currently resides at _____

_____, the sum of _____ dollars ($ _____ ).

      (B) I give to my_____,_____

who currently resides at_____


_____

_____

_____, the sum of_____

dollars ($      ).

                    (C) I give to my _____,_____

who currently resides at _____

_____, the sum of _____

_____ dollars ($   ).

                    (D) I give to my_____,_____

who currently resides at_____

_____, the sum of_____

dollars ($_____).

                    (E) I give to my _____,_____

who currently resides at _____

_____, the sum of _____

dollars ($ _____).

                    (F) I give to my_____,_____

who currently resides at_____

_____, the sum of_____

dollars ($   ).

       FIFTH: All the rest residue and remainder of my estates both real and personal, and wheresoever situated, of which I may have title possession at the time of my death, or to which I may be in any way entitled, which shall be referred to as my "residuary estate," I give to my _____

_____, currently residing at_____. In the event the aforementioned_____ should predecease me or refuse this gift, then I give my residuary estate to my_____,

_____

currently residing at _____

_____

       SIXTH: I direct that the arrangements for the disposition of my body be as follows:

_____

_____

_____

_____

I further direct that my funeral be carried out under the

directions of my executor,_____

      SEVENTH: I direct that no bond or other security shall be required in any jurisdiction of any fiduciary, including a preliminary executor, appointed hereunder for any cause whatsoever, including the advance payment of commissions.

      EIGHTH: I hereby nominate_____

currently residing at _____

_____, as the Executor of this my LAST

WILL AND TESTAMENT. In the event the aforementioned is unable to serve, or ceases to serve,

then I nominate_____

currently residing at_____

_____

as the alternate Executor of this my LAST WILL AND TESTAMENT.

      NINTH: I hereby nominate_____

currently residing at _____

_____,as the Guardian of the person and property

of any minor child of mine. In the event the aforementioned _____,

should become unable to serve as Guardian, then I nominate _____

_____, who resides at_____

_____, as the alternative Guardian of the person

and property of any minor child of mine.

      TENTH: Any property passing hereunder to a minor may be distributed to a guardian of the person or property of such minor appointed in any jurisdiction, or to a custodian of the property of such minor under the Uniform Gifts or Transfers to Minors Act of any State, or to a parent of such minor, or to a person with whom such minor resides or who has control or custody of such minor, as my Executor may determine. If payment is made to a custodian, my Executor may act as the custodian or may select another custodian. The receipt of any such guardian, custodian, or parent or other person to whom any such distribution is made shall completely release and discharge my Executor with respect thereto and my Executor shall be under no further liability, responsibility or application or disposition thereof.

_____

ELEVENTH: My executor and alternate Executor shall have all the express and implied powers granted to Executors by the laws of the state in which probate occurs in effect at the time of my death.

TWELFTH: If any beneficiary shall not survive me, any legacy here under to that beneficiary shall lapse, unless this Will shall provide otherwise.

_____
Testator's Signature

IN WITNESS WHEREOF, I, _____ have to this my LAST WILL AND TESTAMENT, consisting of _____ (___) pages, up to and including this page, subscribed my name at the end hereof this _____ day of _____, 199__.

The foregoing instrument was subscribed, sealed, published and declared by _____, the Testator, as and for (his/her) LAST WILL AND TESTAMENT, in our presence and in the presence of each of us, and we, at the same time, in (his/her) presence and in the presence of each other, having hereunto subscribed our names and residences as attesting witnesses this _____ day of _____, 199__.

_____ residing at _____

_____ residing at _____

_____ residing at _____

_____
Testator

# WITNESS VERIFICATION PAGE

STATE OF _____

COUNTY OF _____

We the undersigned, being duly sworn, depose and say:

1. We witnessed the execution of the foregoing Will, dated _____, 199__, of the Testator _____. Said Testator subscribed said Will at the end thereof at the following address: _____, in our presence. At the time of making such subscription, the said Testator declared such instrument so subscribed by (him/her) to be (his/her) Will, and we thereupon signed our names as witness at the end of said instrument, at the request of said Testator, and in (his/her) presence and in the presence of each other.

2. In the opinion of each of the undersigned:

    (A) The said Testator at the time of executing said instrument was over the age of eighteen (18) years, of sound mind, memory and understanding, and not under any restraint or in any respect incompetent to make a will.

    (B) The said Testator could read, write and converse in the English language and was suffering from no defect of sight, hearing or speech, or from any other physical or mental impairment which would affect (his/her) capacity to make a valid Will.

3. Each of the undersigned was acquainted with said Testator, and we make this affidavit at the request of said Testator.

4. The said instrument was executed by said Testator and each of the undersigned, as witness, under the supervision of the Testator.

_____
Testator:

_____
Witness:

_____
Witness:

_____
Witness:

Severally sworn to before me this _____ day of _____, 19___.

_____
Notary Public

# PROPERTY LIST

Estate of _____

Residing at _____

_____

Date this list was last updated _____

## 1. Real Estate

  a. Residence:

  Address and/or description: _____

  _____

  _____

  Market value: $_____ How value was arrived at

  _____

  Amount of any known mortgage or lien and the name and address of any party which has a mortgage, lien, or other interest in the property:

  _____

  _____

  b. Other interests in real property: Address or description:

  _____

  _____

  Market value: $_____How Value was arrived at:_____

  _____

  Amount of any known mortgage or lien and the name and address of the party who has a mortgage, lien, or other interest in property:

  _____

  _____.

  Name and address of person or persons whom you wish to receive this property upon your death:_____

  _____.

_____

## 2. Stocks, Bonds, Loans owing to the estate

Address and description:_____

_____

Market Value: $_____ How determined:_____

_____.

Name and address of any party with an interest or lien on the property, including a description of the parties' interest:_____

_____

Name and address of person you wish to receive this property upon your death: _____

_____

_____

_____.

Address and description:_____

_____.

Market Value: $_____ How Determined:_____

_____.

Name and address of any party with an interest or lien on the property, including a description of the parties' interest:_____

_____.

Name and address of person you wish to receive this property upon your death:_____

_____

## 3. Life Insurance and Employee Benefits

Type of insurance:_____

Market Value: $_____ How determined:_____

_____

Name of insurance company:_____

Name and address of your insurance broker, or the company representative who handles insurance claims at your company:

_____

_____

If you have borrowed against this policy give an explanation including amount borrowed,

_____

_____

and the location of all related records:_____

_____

    Name and address of all beneficiaries:_____

_____

    Type of insurance or benefit:_____

    Market value: $_____ How Determined:_____

_____

    Name of insurance company:_____

    Name and address of your insurance broker, or the company representative who handles insurance claims at your company:

_____

_____

    If you have borrowed against this policy provide an explanation including the amount borrowed, and the location of all related records:_____

_____

    Name and address of all beneficiaries:_____

_____

## 4. Interests in vehicles

    Type of vehicle:_____

_____

    Vehicle identification number:_____

    Market value: $_____How Determined:_____

_____

    This vehicle insured by:_____

    Name and address of person to whom you desire to inherit this vehicle:_____

_____

    If you have a loan on the vehicle or share ownership with another person, so state, and provide an explanation of such interest including the location of all related records:

_____

_____

    Type of vehicle:_____

_____

_____

_____

Vehicle identification number:_____

Market value: $_____ How Determined:_____

_____

This vehicle insured by:_____

Name and address of person to whom you desire to inherit this vehicle:_____

_____

If you have a loan on the vehicle or share ownership with another person, so state, and provide an explanation of such interest including the location of all related records:

_____

_____

## 5. Bank Accounts

Type of account:_____

Account number:_____

Name and address of Bank:_____

_____

Estimated value:_____

Name and address of any beneficiary or co-owner of account:

_____

_____

If you have a lien or pledge against the account, so state, and provide an explanation of such interest including the location of all documentation related thereto:_____

_____

Type of account:_____

Account number:_____

Name and address of Bank:_____

_____

Estimated value:_____

Name and address of any beneficiary or co-owner of account:

_____

_____

If you have a lien or pledge against the account, so state, and provide an explanation of such interest including the location of all documentation related thereto:_____

## 6. Safety Deposit Boxes

Name and address of the Bank which contains your safety deposit box:
_____
_____

Number of your safety deposit box:_____

Name and address of any party other than yourself with access to this depository:_____
_____

Name and address of person or persons you want to receive contents of the safety deposit box upon your death:_____
_____

## 7. Other property

Description of property:_____
Location of property:_____
Name of person who has possession of property:_____
_____
Name and address of any party who has an interest in the property:_____
_____

Value of property: $_____ How Determined:_____
_____

Location of any documents relating to your ownership of the property:
_____

Name and address of person or persons whom you wish to receive this property upon your death:_____
_____

Description of property:_____
Location of property:_____

Name and address of person who has possession of property:_____

_____

Name and address of any party who has an interest in the property:_____

_____

_____

Value of property: $_____ How Determined:_____

_____

Location of any documents relating to your ownership of the property:
_____

Name and address of person or persons whom you wish to receive this property upon your death:_____

_____

Description of property:_____

Location of property:_____

Name of person who has possession of property:_____

_____

Name and address of any party who has an interest in the property:_____

_____

_____

Value of property: $_____ How Determined:_____

_____

Location of any documents relating to your ownership of the property:
_____

Name and address of person or persons whom you wish to receive this property upon your death:_____

_____

_____

# NOTES

# NOTES

# NOTES

# NOTES

# LAST WILL AND TESTAMENT
# OF

_____

I,_____

residing at_____

_____, in the County of _____

_____, City of _____, State of

_____, do hereby make, publish and declare the following as and for my LAST WILL AND TESTAMENT.

    FIRST:    I hereby revoke any and all wills and codicils by me at any time heretofore made.

    SECOND: I direct my Executor to pay out of my estate as an expense of administration, without apportionment, all estate, death, transfer, succession, inheritance, legacy, and similar taxes by whatever name called, including interest and penalties thereon, which may be assessed or imposed under the laws of any jurisdiction by reason of my death, upon or with respect to any property passing under this my LAST WILL AND TESTAMENT.

    THIRD:    (A) I give_____

_____to my _____

_____, currently residing at

_____

_____.

    (B) I give_____

to my _____, _____

_____, currently residing at _____

_____.

    (C) I give _____

to my _____, _____

_____, currently residing at _____

_____.

    (D) I give _____

to my _____, _____

_____, currently residing at _____

_____

_____.

      (E) I give _____

to my _____, _____

_____, currently residing at _____

_____.

      (F) I give _____

to my _____, _____

_____, currently residing at _____

_____.

      (G) I give _____

to my _____, _____

_____, currently residing at _____

_____.

      (H) I give all (other) tangible personal property owned by me at the time of my death, including but not limited to all articles of personal and household use or ornament, including articles (not effectively disposed of under the foregoing provisions), to my _____, _____

_____, currently residing at _____

_____

_____.

In the event that the aforementioned _____

_____, should predecease me or refuse their gift, then I give all said tangible personal property to my _____, _____

_____, currently residing

at _____

    FOURTH:  (A) I give to my _____, _____

who currently resides at _____

_____, the sum of _____ dollars ($ _____ ).

      (B) I give to my _____, _____

who currently resides at _____

_____

_____, the sum of_____
dollars ($      ).

      (C) I give to my _____,_____
who currently resides at _____
_____, the sum of _____
_____ dollars ($   ).

      (D) I give to my_____,_____
who currently resides at_____
_____, the sum of_____
dollars ($_____).

      (E) I give to my _____,_____
who currently resides at _____
_____, the sum of _____
dollars ($ _____).

      (F) I give to my_____,_____
who currently resides at_____
_____, the sum of_____
dollars ($   ).

  FIFTH: All the rest residue and remainder of my estates both real and personal, and wheresoever situated, of which I may have title possession at the time of my death, or to which I may be in any way entitled, which shall be referred to as my "residuary estate," I give to my _____
_____, currently residing at_____. In the event the aforementioned_____ should predecease me or refuse this gift, then I give my residuary estate to my_____,
_____
currently residing at _____
_____

  SIXTH: I direct that the arrangements for the disposition of my body be as follows:

_____

_____

_____

I further direct that my funeral be carried out under the

directions of my executor,_____

      SEVENTH: I direct that no bond or other security shall be required in any jurisdiction of any fiduciary, including a preliminary executor, appointed hereunder for any cause whatsoever, including the advance payment of commissions.

      EIGHTH: I hereby nominate_____

currently residing at _____

_____, as the Executor of this my LAST

WILL AND TESTAMENT. In the event the aforementioned is unable to serve, or ceases to serve,

then I nominate_____

currently residing at_____

_____

as the alternate Executor of this my LAST WILL AND TESTAMENT.

      NINTH: I hereby nominate_____

currently residing at _____

_____,as the Guardian of the person and property

of any minor child of mine. In the event the aforementioned _____,

should become unable to serve as Guardian, then I nominate _____

_____, who resides at_____

_____, as the alternative Guardian of the person

and property of any minor child of mine.

      TENTH: Any property passing hereunder to a minor may be distributed to a guardian of the person or property of such minor appointed in any jurisdiction, or to a custodian of the property of such minor under the Uniform Gifts or Transfers to Minors Act of any State, or to a parent of such minor, or to a person with whom such minor resides or who has control or custody of such minor, as my Executor may determine. If payment is made to a custodian, my Executor may act as the custodian or may select another custodian. The receipt of any such guardian, custodian, or parent or other person to whom any such distribution is made shall completely release and discharge my Executor with respect thereto and my Executor shall be under no further liability, responsibility or application or disposition thereof.

_____

ELEVENTH: My executor and alternate Executor shall have all the express and implied powers granted to Executors by the laws of the state in which probate occurs in effect at the time of my death.

TWELFTH: If any beneficiary shall not survive me, any legacy here under to that beneficiary shall lapse, unless this Will shall provide otherwise.

_____
Testator's Signature

IN WITNESS WHEREOF, I, _____ have to this my LAST WILL AND TESTAMENT, consisting of _____ (____) pages, up to and including this page, subscribed my name at the end hereof this _____ day of _____, 199__.

The foregoing instrument was subscribed, sealed, published and declared by _____, the Testator, as and for (his/her) LAST WILL AND TESTAMENT, in our presence and in the presence of each of us, and we, at the same time, in (his/her) presence and in the presence of each other, having hereunto subscribed our names and residences as attesting witnesses this _____ day of _____, 199__.

_____ residing at _____

_____ residing at _____

_____ residing at _____

_____
Testator

# WITNESS VERIFICATION PAGE

STATE OF _____

COUNTY OF_____

    We the undersigned, being duly sworn, depose and say:

    1.   We witnessed the execution of the foregoing Will, dated _____, 199__, of the Testator _____. Said Testator subscribed said Will at the end thereof at the following address: _____, in our presence. At the time of making such subscription, the said Testator declared such instrument so subscribed by (him/her) to be (his/her) Will, and we thereupon signed our names as witness at the end of said instrument, at the request of said Testator, and in (his/her) presence and in the presence of each other.

    2.   In the opinion of each of the undersigned:

        (A)  The said Testator at the time of executing said instrument was over the age of eighteen (18) years, of sound mind, memory and understanding, and not under any restraint or in any respect incompetent to make a will.

        (B)  The said Testator could read, write and converse in the English language and w suffering from no defect of sight, hearing or speech, or from any other physical or mental impairment which would affect (his/her) capacity to make a valid Will.

    3.   Each of the undersigned was acquainted with said Testator, and we make this affida at the request of said Testator.

    4.   The said instrument was executed by said Testator and each of the undersigned, as witness, under the supervision of the Testator.

_____
Testator:

_____
Witness:

_____
Witness:

_____
Witness:

Severally sworn to before me this
_____day of _____, 19___.

_____
Notary Public

# PROPERTY LIST

Estate of _____

Residing at _____

_____

Date this list was last updated _____

## 1. Real Estate

a. Residence:

Address and/or description: _____

_____

_____

Market value: $_____ How value was arrived at

_____

Amount of any known mortgage or lien and the name and address of any party which has a mortgage, lien, or other interest in the property:

_____

_____

b. Other interests in real property: Address or description:

_____

_____

Market value: $_____How Value was arrived at:_____

_____

Amount of any known mortgage or lien and the name and address of the party who has a mortgage, lien, or other interest in property:

_____

_____.

Name and address of person or persons whom you wish to receive this property upon your death:_____

_____.

2. **Stocks, Bonds, Loans** owing to the estate

   Address and description:_____

   _____

   Market Value: $_____How determined:_____

   _____.

   Name and address of any party with an interest or lien on the property, including a description of the parties' interest:_____

   _____

   Name and address of person you wish to receive this property upon your death: _____

   _____

   _____

   _____.

   Address and description:_____

   _____.

   Market Value: $_____How Determined:_____

   _____.

   Name and address of any party with an interest or lien on the property, including a description of the parties' interest:_____

   _____.

   Name and address of person you wish to receive this property upon your death:_____

   _____

   _____

3. **Life Insurance and Employee Benefits**

   Type of insurance:_____

   Market Value: $_____ How determined:_____

   _____

   Name of insurance company:_____

   Name and address of your insurance broker, or the company representative who handles insurance claims at your company:

   _____

   _____

   If you have borrowed against this policy give an explanation including amount borrowed,

   _____

and the location of all related records:_____

    Name and address of all beneficiaries:_____

    Type of insurance or benefit:_____

    Market value: $_____ How Determined:_____

    Name of insurance company:_____

    Name and address of your insurance broker, or the company representative who handles insurance claims at your company:

    If you have borrowed against this policy provide an explanation including the amount borrowed, and the location of all related records:_____

    Name and address of all beneficiaries:_____

## 4. Interests in vehicles

    Type of vehicle:_____

    Vehicle identification number:_____

    Market value: $_____ How Determined:_____

    This vehicle insured by:_____

    Name and address of person to whom you desire to inherit this vehicle:_____

    If you have a loan on the vehicle or share ownership with another person, so state, and provide an explanation of such interest including the location of all related records:_____

    Type of vehicle:_____

_____

Vehicle identification number:_____

Market value: $_____ How Determined:_____

_____

This vehicle insured by:_____

Name and address of person to whom you desire to inherit this
vehicle:_____

_____

If you have a loan on the vehicle or share ownership with another person, so state, and provide an explanation of such interest including the location of all related records:

_____

_____

## 5. Bank Accounts

Type of account:_____

Account number:_____

Name and address of Bank:_____

_____

Estimated value:_____

Name and address of any beneficiary or co-owner of account:

_____

_____

If you have a lien or pledge against the account, so state, and provide an explanation of such interest including the location of all documentation related thereto:_____

_____

Type of account:_____

Account number:_____

Name and address of Bank:_____

_____

Estimated value:_____

Name and address of any beneficiary or co-owner of account:

_____

_____

_____

_____

If you have a lien or pledge against the account, so state, and provide an explanation

of such interest including the location of all documentation related thereto:_____

## 6. Safety Deposit Boxes

Name and address of the Bank which contains your safety deposit box:

_____

_____

Number of your safety deposit box:_____

Name and address of any party other than yourself with access to this

depository:_____

_____

Name and address of person or persons you want to receive contents of the safety

deposit box upon your death:_____

_____

## 7. Other property

Description of property:_____

Location of property:_____

Name of person who has possession of property:_____

_____

Name and address of any party who has an interest in the property:_____

_____

_____

Value of property: $_____ How Determined:_____

_____

Location of any documents relating to your ownership of the property:

_____

Name and address of person or persons whom you wish to receive this property upon

your death:_____

_____

Description of property:_____

Location of property:_____

_____

Name and address of person who has possession of property:_____

Name and address of any party who has an interest in the property:_____

Value of property: $_____ How Determined:_____

Location of any documents relating to your ownership of the property:

Name and address of person or persons whom you wish to receive this property upon your death:_____

Description of property:_____
Location of property:_____
Name of person who has possession of property:_____

Name and address of any party who has an interest in the property:_____

Value of property: $_____ How Determined:_____

Location of any documents relating to your ownership of the property:

Name and address of person or persons whom you wish to receive this property upon your death:_____

# NOTES

# NOTES

# NOTES

# NOTES